skiing

THE SKIING DICTIONARY

British Library Cataloguing in Publication Data

Dunstan, Keith
  The skiing dictionary.
  1. Skis and skiing – Anecdotes, facetiae,
satire, etc.
  I. Title
  796.93'0207   GV854.3

ISBN 0-7153-9141-0

© 1987 Text: Keith Dunstan
Illustrations: Jeff Hook

First published in Australia by Sun Books 1987
First published in Great Britain by David & Charles 1987

Printed in Hong Kong
for David & Charles Publishers plc
Brunel House   Newton Abbot   Devon

skiing

THE SKIING DICTIONARY
BY KEITH DUNSTAN
ILLUSTRATED BY JEFF HOOK

DAVID & CHARLES
Newton Abbot   London

ABOMINABLE SNOWMAN...

A

Abfahrt	We know it all too well, and it is particularly regrettable on a two-man bobsled. *Abfahrt*, of course, is the German term for a downhill ski run.
Ability	Being able to sleep and drive home at the same time.
Abominable Snowman	Vile, healthy creature who shrieks 'there's powder' and wants to be on the snow at 6.30 am or: One who skis better than you do and says so. Thinks he owns the slope. Uses the T-bar for more than transport. Has been to more resorts than he has bought drinks.
Adiabatic Lapse Rate	Rate of air cooling as one ascends the mountain. There is also an alpiatic rise rate. This is the increase in prices as one ascends the mountain.
Aerial Turns	Starting to feel faint with excitement when your aircraft approaches the ski area.
Aficionado	One who has mirrored sun glasses, as many sets of skis as he has cars, wears Goretex gear or Dachstein boots, has Salomon bindings, knows the Redfords very well because he met them at Aspen last December and members of the Royal Family, of course. (He always sees them very quietly at St Moritz.)
Akya	High-speed cosy sled, propelled by the finest and most dexterous skiers on the mountain. For a quick, slick trip back to the lodge all you need is a broken leg.
Anti-Freeze	Gentle, warm, loving massage.

Après-Ski	Activity which requires more stamina, style and brilliance of movement than actually skiing. Those who are truly adept at après-ski don't need to ski at all.
Arthritis	Disease sent by the Almighty to remind you of seasons and breaks you might have forgotten.
Asprin	Obligatory drug for turning après-ski into ante-ski.

B

Backpacking	Carrying on your back all those things you are unlikely to use until you get back home.
Balaclava	Garment worn in armed hold-ups and when going incognito down the mountain.
Bankruptcy	A lovely warm winter.
Basket	Plastic piece on ski stocks designed to prevent the harpooning of other skiers by more than four centimetres.
Beginner	Innocent who has not been told that he or she will spend thousands on equipment and beautiful gear, more thousands on getting there and being there, and that for at least the next twenty years the mind never again will be on ground level. True happiness will be found only in the arms of the snow god.

BALACLAVA...

BLADDER...

Benjanees	The most-used phrase on the mountain, slightly ahead of 'Uh, wotcha doing later?'
Bindings	Back in the old days they were literally just that, primitive straps which tied your boots on to the boards. Now they are ingenious devices of incredible complexity, designed to release instantly in moments of peril. Every year competing manufacturers invent better, more brilliant devices which you feel it is compulsory to purchase, so the children have to go without clothes for another twelve months since your fancy bindings cost as much as a summer holiday in France. Sometimes you wish progress would go back to 1934.
Bladder	Difficult, contrary item at any time. But if you really want to spend money, purchase the expensive boots in which they pump liquid foam or putty into an inner bladder, which conforms perfectly to the shape of your foot. Works like a dream until you want to do something human like wiggle your toes.
Blizzard	Something which always happens when you are battling to get there. Something which never happens when you don't want to get back from there.
Boards	One always 'gets out on the boards'. Not to be confused with bawds, which also are readily available.
Bone	Absurdly brittle substance, part of the human skeletal frame, which cracks easily when misdirected at speed aboard two pieces of timber.

Boots	They used to be simple, lace-up affairs like grandfather wore. Now they look as if they were designed for walking on Saturn. It is death to be seen in black. They have to be cherry red, blue or hazard-yellow. They have quick release buckles, cable tensioners, electric thermo pads, and more controls than your high-fi. You can pay hundreds a pair. Get out on the snow and they still hurt like hell.
Bum	Portion of anatomy, usually well-cushioned, exquisitely designed for falling upon.
Bum Bag	Storage spot for make-up, hanky, money, brandy flask, chocolate bars. Polite people prefer to call it a posterior receptacle.
Bumps (1)	Prominences on the head regarded as indicators of intelligence and character by phrenologists. On the snow, they are regarded as examples of intelligence and character if you handle them still in one piece.
Bumps (2)	Prominences prominent enough to make an impression on a parka.
Bunk	Device designed for straightening backs, laughably used as a bed.
Bunny	Creature who performs better by far in bistro, bunk or bar than on the boards.

Bum...

CAUGHT SHORT...

C

Calisthenics	Methods for creating agony before going skiing, to prevent agony afterwards.

Calories	Four out of five intelligent people ski for its healthy slimming qualities. Compare 60 minutes of:
	    Desk-sitting: 20 calories.
	    Standing at a drafting board–30 calories.
	    Hiking–130 calories.
	    Alpine hiking–200 calories.
	    Cycling–200–300 calories.
	    Skiing–500–900 calories.
	    Après-skiing–minus 1000–2000 calories.

Canting	Talking at the bar.
Caught Short	Jet-fighter pilots, parachutists, deep-sea divers, conductors of Beethoven's Ninth Symphony and skiers find the passing of water something that is conducted only with difficulty.
Chains	Scientists have put a man on the moon but still they have not invented anything more convenient than horrid tyre chains. The time to observe skiers in all their rich eloquence is at that pregnant moment when they bend down, hands and knees on the snow, to attach their chains. You will learn to express yourself colourfully in twenty different languages.
Chair Lift	The romantic side of skiing: chair-lifts, T-bars, almost everything is built for two.

CHAIR LIFTS...

CHILD...

Child	Unnerving, irritating creature, who can go down the slopes with twice the aplomb and at four times the speed that you can.
Chill Factor	Receiving no encouragement from the dear companion who seemed so friendly on the T-bar.
Christie	The whole family of turns, and for the deeply devoted, it just has to be the name of their female first-born. The male, of course is Mark, short for telemark.
Club	Joyous get-together of all the people you have been avoiding throughout the summer.
Colour	Once upon a time the better the skier, the duller he looked. One dressed in dark blue or black. Now there is intense competition to look as vulgar as possible with colours that outshine a TV test pattern. Unquestionably the reason so many skiers wear dark glasses.
Compass	Gadget you bring out only when you realise you are irretrievably lost.
Confusion	The trouble with skiing, like filming *Ben Hur*, is getting started. There's the problem of sorting out your parka, pants, inners, outers, beanie, boots, socks, sun glasses, gloves, skis, bindings, stocks, tow tickets, sun cream, lip salve, scarf . . . By the time you have got the whole act to the ski lift it's time to come home again.
Conventional Entry	God really meant that we should do things in the normal way. Conventional entry is getting into your ski boots via the top. (*See* Rear Entry.)

CHRISTIE...

CRUTCHES...

Corn	Spring snow. When the stuff starts to go like rice bubbles in warm milk you know it is time for the homing pigeon to return to things horrid: bitumen, traffic lights and (shudder) desks.
Cornice	The marvellous overhang of snow you get on a steep slope. They even develop their own Doric, Ionic and incredible Corinthian beauty—something to think about when a cornice collapses and you are left in a Corinthian heap.
Credit Cards	Actually, they should be called debt cards. You spend all summer paying for what went on all winter.
Crevasse	Instant, long-term accommodation for skiers.
Cross-Country	Ingenious method for getting away from crowds, from queues, from monotonous up-and-down slopes, from penury on ski tows . . . and for getting lost.
Crud	Things you hear around the hut, particularly from 11 pm to midnight.
Crutches	Useful devices to have on hand to save one the humiliation of getting out on the snow.

D

Daffy	Aerial-style manoeuvre with legs outstretched diagonally. Actually it applies to almost everything on the mountain.

Dampening	Has everything to do with the flexibility and the ride that your skis give you. The more horizontal riding you do, the damper you will get.
Day Ticket	An item almost anyone can afford after saving up for a month. For a season ticket you get a bank overdraft.
Double Cross	The ultimate disaster, crossing your legs and your skis at the same time.
Downhill	It takes six hours drive to get to the mountain. It takes an hour-and-a-half to get your gear in shape. You queue for half an hour to get on the ski lift. It takes another 10 minutes to get to the top. The trip down takes 45 seconds.
Dry Ski Slope	Surface made of artificial fibre matting, sometimes inside, sometimes outside. It is here that you get your summer instruction in temperatures like 40 degrees celsius. You have dreams of glory that what you learn here magically will convert into beautiful action on powder snow. Actually it is like receiving instruction from Minnie Mouse on how to handle Brigitte Bardot.
Drying Room	Breath-taking area where nothing new is ever found again and all gear changes hands.

E

Ear Muffs	Articles for protecting one from gossip in ski queues.
Eating Snow	Colloquial expression to describe the power dive, or vertical approach to skiing.

EGG POSITION (SEE ALSO 'EDGE')...

23

Edge	Sharp piece of metal on each side of your ski designed for carving ice. Also the extremely embarrassing finish of the mountain.
Edge Hold	It comes at about 11 pm. It's learning how to hold on to the edge of the bar without actually swaying.
Egg Position	For some it is the high-speed downhill crouch, for others it is sitting down hoping someone else will cook your breakfast.
Entrepreneur	As he accepts your cheque, he tells you with tears in his eyes of the awful difficulties of operating in the snow, the vagaries of the weather, the multiple costs of getting things up the mountain, the horrid brevity of the season, the taxes of shire and government, of pending bankruptcy. Yet everything will be bigger and twice the size next season.
Euphoria	It comes every so often, that super high. For once the snow is pure fresh powder, you have the mountain almost to yourself, your gear is actually working, you have just done four sensational turns and there is a 90 per cent chance you will get to the bottom in one piece.
Every Which Way	White sky, white snow, and trying to work out which way up you are.
Extremities	Areas you are not aware of until you get the feeling they are about to fall off.

F

Faith	Looking up at that hideously thin wire on the chair lift and believing it will hold you up there for ever.
Fall Line	The shortest and most direct way by which gravity can put you in an upended position.
Fanatic	One who does 12 hours driving for every six on the snow.
Fashion	You can spend thousands on your parka, on your fancy Goretex pants, on a powder suit, on goggles, on matching gloves, on a matching headband, and the beauty of it is, the whole lot will be out-of-date next season.
Fit	You can throw fits or you can achieve fit in ski gear. Neither is ever very satisfactory.
Flat	It is interesting how quickly you discover so little of the world is flat. Interesting too how those damn skis start to wander when you think it is impossible.
Flipping	Doing somersaults. The record is a triple somersault although attempts are being made to do a quadruple. (Anyone can do a somersault if they go over a precipice.)
Flying	Ski flying is achieved by jumping from hills in excess of 90 metres. In other words you do 20 years of training and buy equipment worth thousands to get in a position where you don't need it.

FLIPPING...

Fondue	Method devised for reducing good cheese to a hot, treacly, mouth-burning mess.
Four-Wheel Drive	Vehicle designed to match your fearless, outdoors, go-anywhere, venturesome personality, even if it is used for that purpose only .05 per cent of the time, and costs you the earth and half the mountain in petrol.
Freestyle	No such thing on the mountain unless you have a friendly sponsor or a rich boyfriend.
Frost Bite	Season's ticket.

G

Geeeeeeeeezus	Standard exclamation made when confronted with the advanced skier's slope.
Gloves	Garments which not only never keep the tips of your fingers warm but are designed so that it is impossible to do up a zip without taking them off. (Nor can you remember at which lodge you left them last night.)
Gluwein	Ritual après-ski drink of the seducer. Cheap, bulk red wine allegedly made drinkable by heating and spicing. Makes you see double and feel single.
Gondola	Little cabin job on ski lift for two, or even four passengers. Some are equipped with heating and all comforts. Eventually there will be such progress skiers won't have to venture into the cold, crude atmosphere at all.

GLUWEIN...

GUMBOOTS...

Good Week-end	Stretching things a little, like Tuesday right through to Monday.
Grass	Herbage upon which the incredibly devoted actually ski in the summer months. Originally invented to persecute the home gardener.
Gravity	As mentioned by Einstein and the Theory of Relativity, this enormous force accounts for the fortunes of the ski lift proprietors.
Gum Boots (Wellingtons)	Devices for tramping through deep snow and thus getting filled with water.

H

Happiness	Taking your feet out of the blocks of concrete they have been in all day, putting on dry warm socks, and discovering you can still feel something there after all.
Happy Hour	Time for recording lies about heroic achievements during battle.
Hard Pack	Could be hard-packed snow, but more likely your pack is carrying too many bottles.
Head	Cranium repository for beanie and other exotica of the home-knit variety.
Helicopter (1)	Rich man's ski tow.
Helicopter (2)	Aerial freestyle manoeuvre with a hotdogging 360-degree turn. Splendid way of getting rid of unnecessary skiers.

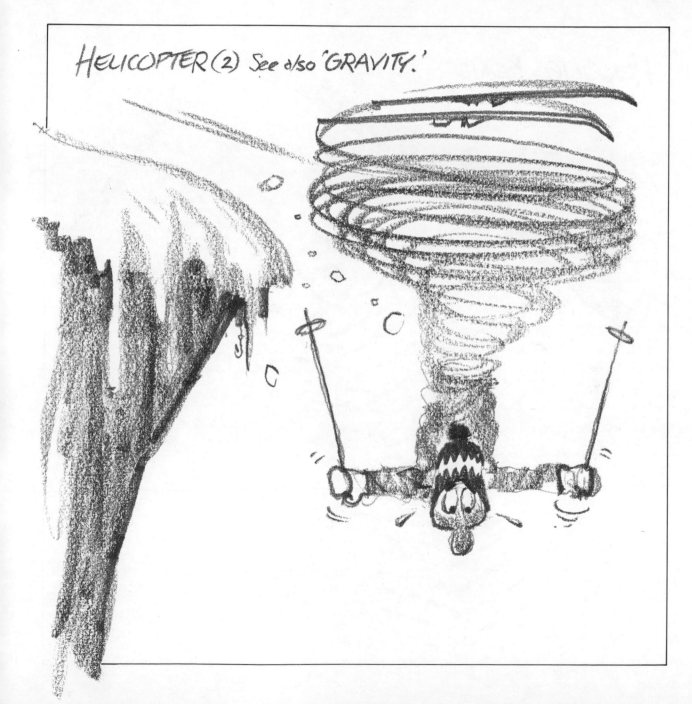

Heli-Skiing	Being deposited on top of a mountain or glacier by a helicopter with only one possible way of getting home again.
Helmet	Safety equipment insufficiently worn by daring skiers. Most of them think Helmut is the divine looking character who arrives every year from the Jungfrau.
Herring-Bone	Like the cross, the rack and the thumb screw, an old fashioned symbol of torture. You see victims on every hill.
High Country	Only part of the world where, through the ingenious nature of the weather, you can get sunburn and frost-bite at the same time.
Hire	Paying the mountain for a whole range of gear that doesn't fit and you still have to give back.
Hood	Attachment to parka designed to be filled with rain and snow.
Hotdogger	The skiting bastard who goes past doing fancy tricks while you are lying horizontal on the snow.
Hypothermia	Symptoms: Fits of shivering, fear, foggy speech, extreme fatigue, fainting, funny behaviour. Often caused by presentation of the accommodation bill at the end of the holiday.

I

Ice	Hideous stuff that settles solid on your windscreen and makes skiing hazardous. Yet formed into cubes and covered with Scotch it can be passably useful.
Independent Leg Action	A turn using one leg as main motivating force and the other as balance. Frankly, it is the independent action of the skis that causes all the trouble.
Instructor	He skis divinely, he has a voice like Charles Boyer, a gorgeous sun tan, yet he hasn't seen a summer for 16 years. Despite this hardship he's marvellously sympathetic to the female beginners.
Irony	Breaking your ankle on the steps of the ski lodge.

J

Jeans	Antique garment still worn on the snow. Very trendy. It's hard to pick whether the wearer came up on yesterday's bus, or whether he is a genuine veteran, skilled at upmanship, who can remember when skis were made of hickory.
Jet Turn	Sensitive display one puts on for the airline company when one discovers one is in Vienna and one's skis are in Tel Aviv or Singapore or Sydney.
Job	Fund-raising acitivity to get you on the snow.

JUMPING...

Jumpers	Heavy wool, ribs, cables, intricate design invented by women during long black winters, with the object of disguising any reasonable shape.
Jumping	Learning how to go in head first from a greater height.

K

Kamikaze	One whose magnificence of courage and speed on the slope is in inverse proportion to his brains and skill.
Kick Turn	Tantrum.
Knee	Complex hinge which connects thigh bone to the shin bone. Clearly, when God designed the knee, He never thought of the appalling strains and leverage imposed by wearing two long pieces of board. There's not much you can do with a skier who has gone at the knees except prop him against a bar.
Knee Control	Sharp slap of the hand used to deter feelers under the table.

L

Lean	The key to the entire problem. Keeping your shoulders ahead of your hips. Very good training for this can be acquired in the bar.

Lessons	Daily session in which you pay large sums of money to take turns.
Lifts	Contrivances designed to lift skiers from one level to another and keep them at the same time in a state of penury.
Ligament	Band of tough fibrous tissue which holds bones together. One knows nothing about them until one takes up skiing. Then one becomes expert.
Loipe	Marked and prepared for cross-country skiers. (Cross-country was always free but then they found a way of making you pay.)
Love	Means: Devotedly waxing somebody else's skis. Picking up a fallen creature from the snow. Herring-boning back up the slope for her lost mitten. Trying to find her lodge at midnight in a blizzard. Calling her again when you get back home.

M

Man-Made Snow	Powdered money. Like heroin, suicide notes, armed hold-ups, and letters to the headmaster, committed only in times of desperation.
Mashed Potatoes	Slush or porridge. Terms to describe heavy wet snow and the food you get at the lodge.

LESSONS...

Moguls...

Masochism	Still wanting to do it when you are wet, frost-bitten, sore in every muscle, when you have fallen over for the ninety-third time and spent all your money.
Moguls	Originally monsters whose feats of cruelty spread terror through Asia. Here they are equally cruel man-made monsters on the snow. Regrettably too, like some chocolates, they have hard centres.
Mountain	Large excrescence on the earth which supports 10,000 or more strange people in frigid conditions, who then desert it as soon as the weather becomes comfortable.
Muscles	Traction devices, some of which you may never formally have met or heard of until the day after you went skiing. Then they created more protests than a builders' union.

N

Nursery	Terrifying area where nobody knows how to get out of each other's way.
Nut	One who:

Keeps his skis by his bed, sleeps with them, and constantly, lovingly, strokes them with wax.

Never takes the ski racks off his car.

Has a SUMMER IS HELL—WINTER I LIVE bumper sticker.

Likes to stomp round the house in ski boots to keep his feet in shape.

Has a perpetual lean forward 15 degrees off vertical, and every so often like a nervous twitch, does an imaginary kick turn.

O

Office	Place where one sits from Monday to Friday recovering one's strength and pining for hideous weather that will provide sunshine and perfect powder snow for next week-end on the slopes.
Off Piste	Skiing areas off the marked slopes and trails. Not to be confused with piste off. (*See* Piste.)

ORTHOPAEDIC SURGEON...

Ohmigod	Useful expression when your skis are gathering speed straight down hill and there is no possibility of being able to stop.
Old Age	1. When you think 9.30 is a good time to go to bed. 2. When you can remember lace-up boots and ski trousers with fly buttons. 3. When you think winters were longer and provided better snow in the old days. 4. When you think ski instructors look too young to know anything. 5. When you like to corner a young creature and tell of the harrowing times back in the forties, how there were no tows, no shops, no car parks. You walked up the mountain carrying all your gear, all your provisions. There were heroes who even carried a dozen bottles or kegs on their backs . . . 6. And you are truly old when you are terrified of having a second beer for fear of having to venture out of your warm bed at 3 am.
Orienteering	Planned confusion of skiers with aid of a map and a compass.
Orthopaedic Surgeon	One who has a warm, friendly love for all skiers, and particularly their bones. Wouldn't dream of doing it himself. His Mercedes will never grow old.

P

Parallel
You learn to do parallel turns and parallel step turns. Indeed, like running a good railway, life is never so healthy when the lines cease to be parallel.

Parka
Clever garment that hides everything underneath and makes all skiers look the same shape and sex.

Parking Space
You drive 650 kilometres away from those horrid city parking meters yet still you can't find a place to park the darned thing, and if you do it costs twice as much as a fancy parking area under shelter in the city.

Perspicacious Skier
One who has the foresight of a squirrel. He ships all his grog into the hut two months before the first snow fall.

Pick Up
It is an unwritten law that you don't pick up the fallen. They should get up themselves, with notable exceptions:
1. Broken bones.
2. They are carrying the brandy.
3. If they are young and very beautiful.

Pile Driver
Colourful name for colourful manoeuvre: diving into the snow head-first.

Piste
A marked trail and not to be confused with piste or even half-piste. The most dangerous pistes trail through the lodges, which could leave you piste out of your mind. (*See* Off Piste.)

Poma
Device for lifting you up the mountain, very dangerous to the eternal fertility.

PISTE...

POWDER SNOW...

Powderhound	Genuine devotee. Will sacrifice anything, mother, father, job or bank balance to get on the snow. Loves his skis even more than sex.
Powder Snow	The magical glittering perfect conditions which the TV girls coo over in their weather reports. By the time you get there rain has turned it into slush.

Q

Queue	Arrangement anything up to 200 metres long created at ski lifts for the purpose of exchanging gossip and sexual assignations.
Quiet	Maybe it cost a mint to get here, but this is what you pay for. No traffic noises, no horrid air or sound pollution, no police sirens, not a thing that is an assault to eye or ear, just the magical zssss of your skis.

R

Rain	Regrettable material which should be distributed only to farmers and city people insufficiently enlightened to come up to the snow.
Rear Entry	Subject to be approached with great delicacy. On the snow it is the method for getting into the new fancy-style boots. (*See* Conventional Entry.)

RED-FACE DIVISION...

Red-Face Division	1. Doing a nose dive even before you get on the T-bar. 2. Watching a lonely ski skidding forever down the slope. 3. A young thing taking pity and helping you up. 4. Dropping a pole from 50 metres up on the ski lift. 5. Knowing your car is four metres under hard snow and guess who locked the keys inside.
Release Binding	Powderhound leave from a spouse for a good weekend.
Rich Person	Someone who winters at Thredbo, then winters at Vale, Aspen or the Jungfrau and hasn't seen a summer since Princess Margaret wore bikinis.
Rocks	Objects made for putting interesting new edges on your skis.
Roller Skis	Skis with wheels, so that you can continue your Nordic masochism on hard roads during the summer.
Roof Rack	Something you should always have on your Porsche, complete with fittings for two pairs of skis. (Gives a sense of style even if you can't ski.)
Run	Narrow, steep strip where large numbers of skiers are concentrated with the greatest possibility of personal collision.

S

Sacrifice	Getting your gear down to an agonised 20 kilos for the world tour. Supreme sacrifice: Taking your ski boots and leaving behind 20 pairs of pretty shoes.
Sago	Combination of snow and hail. Like sago on a boarding house plate, it is a great test of character.
Salopette	Bib and brace overall. Very trendy garment on the slopes. Once it was the symbol of the working man, the carpenter and the plumber—which is exactly as it should be. It is the carpenters and the plumbers who can afford to go skiing.
School Holidays	Brief periods of trauma during the year, usually organised when the least possible snow is available.
Schuss	A term for trying to quieten your partner after he has gone down a hole.
Sexism	You meet someone wonderful on the T-bar then up on the mountain he or she deserts you, and contemptuously moves off into the haze like an Olympic gold medallist.
Short Skis	Like Mercedes, boxes of matches and ski pants, they have become smaller with the years. The shorties are called ski skates and have several advantages: they are less bulky, easier to ski upon and if you have a Rolls-Royce maybe you won't even have to sully it with a ski rack.

SHORT SKIS...

Side Slip	Oh yes, you flatten your skis against the slope and, with an elegant grace, move in a traverse style down the slope—that is until superior forces take over.
Single Ski	Clever system for making skiing twice as hard as on double skis.
Ski Brakes	U-shaped spring clips which theoretically stop that ultimate embarrassment—your ski shooting off on its independent way down the slope. Other ski brakes: trees, huts, rocks, and of course, humans.
Skiing	Uncertain locomotion on two thin boards conducted at the most frigid time of year with object of going downhill so that you can come up again.
Skins	Type of skin suit made of neoprene. For its full majesty it should be purchased one size smaller than one's own skin.
Skis	Simple devices for descending hills covered with solidified moisture. Constructed with airflow hoods, anti-vibration lead-shot capsules, diamond-stone finished edges, negative bevel, fibreglass laminates, dampening rubber layers, aluminium, carbon fibre, kevlar . . . and anyone can buy them at a price!
Slalom	Game where you keep hitting poles. Giant slalom: it's a steeper and longer hill and you hit the poles at a greater speed.
Sleeping Bag	Mobile sleeping device, hell to get into, hell to get out of when you want to go to the bathroom at 4 am and useful for sex only in the most supremely agile and dedicated cases.

Snow	Atmospheric vapour frozen into ice crystals, falling to earth in light, white flakes. The damned stuff always comes down to perfection the week when you are not there.
Snow Ball	Humorous device which provides the maximum entertainment when you are doing the throwing.
Snow Blind	Comes in various forms: Like the Arctic explorer you have had too much whiteness for too long. You are a skiing nut to the point of tedium. So blind in your passion to the activity you don't talk about anything else. You are having such a good time, you are blind every day. Usually from 10 am on.
Snow Blower	Machine for making moguls which would dwarf even Genghis Khan.
Snow Grooming	Returning it all to its wondrous pristine glory the following morning. With some bucks and bunnies this is not so easy.
Snow Drift	Lovely passionate this-is-forever relationship up on the mountain which lasts perhaps 24 hours back in the city.
Snowline	The point where your wife says: 'You would have been smarter if you had put on chains when I suggested it.'
Snowmobile	Man, by superb ingenuity, can now put the internal combustion engine out on the snow, the very thing you came to the mountains to avoid.

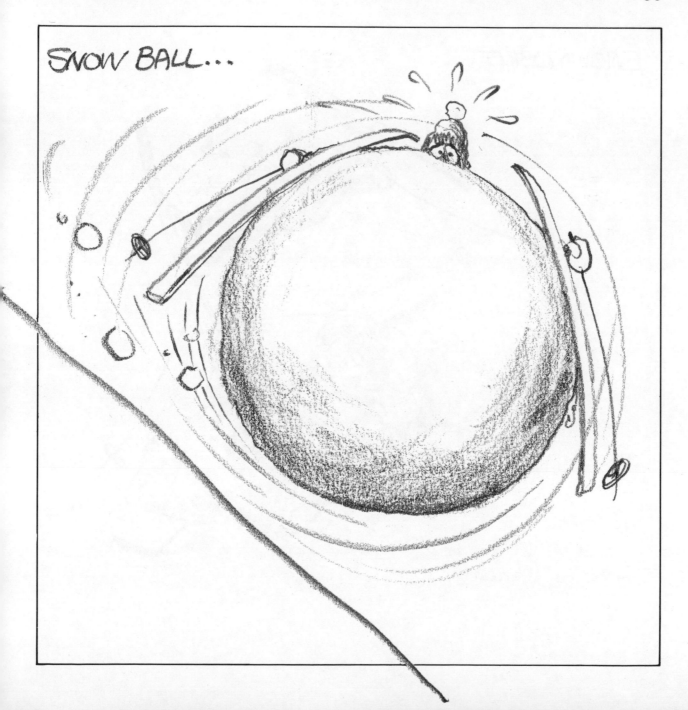

SNOW BALL...

SNOWMOBILE...

Snowplough	Extremely primitive form of turn where one ski is placed at a dramatic angle—one learns quickly the spectacular result of putting one on top of the other.
Space Blanket	Blanket large enough to provide multi-fun in the one bunk.
Spade	Crude device which you keep in the back of the car to dig out the same car when you can't find it.
Sponsor	Remember the time when the mountain was pure and sacrosanct? Now we have the sponsor, the firm which pays. His name appears on every man-made object, every flag, every wall, and every human chest.
Spring	Helmut, Heidi, Hans, Heinz and Helga already have departed for a cooler climate. There are signs up that only two tows are operating. Dramatic runs like Fanny's Finish are sloppy by three o'clock and at nine in the morning they are pure ice. Alas, you'll have to get out of here and do some regrettably necessitous things, like earning money.
Stamina	Leaving the office at 5 pm, driving up to the snow-fields, returning home late on Sunday night and being fit and ready to sleep at the office at 9 am.
Stance	Very important. One must always have the right stance, particularly in the bar, where one takes stances. (At the richer resorts you will find those right stances somewhat to the right of the Louis XIV.)
Stem	This is the beginning: the outward fanning movement of the ski to start the stem christie turn—the launching of the entire catastrophe. (*See* Christie.)

SPADE

STANCE...

STOCK...

Stock	If you are utterly down to earth it is a stick, in America it is more likely to be a pole, in Germany, it is a stock. If you want to show a little bit of upmanship in France it is a baton. The ultimate upmanship is not to use them at all. A stock is a useful device: 1. To stop you falling over. 2. For holding you up when exhausted. 3. For pointing out interesting sights on the snow.
Stopping	A difficult operation, both during ski and after ski.
Stretch	One time skiers wore gear like military riding trousers. Now they have stretch material which makes males and females look remarkably like males and females.
Summer	Awful period when the impecunious and the non-Olympian have to endure warm sun, warm sand, the smell of fresh-cut grass, screech of cicadas, bikinis, mosquitoes, and a whole lot of dreaming.
Summit	In the old days it used to be a perfect thing, an apex, the peak of the mountain. Now it means a conference where nothing ever happens.
Sun Glasses	These are like your car keys—the darned objects that you can never find—but they could be the most vital item when finally you get out on the snow. They hold your eyes in.
Sun Tan	Decoration which the nice people acquire all the year round moving from sand to powder. The interesting achievement is to acquire it all over.
Suspense	Sitting in the car park praying for the engine to kick over after you have turned the ignition key.

SUMMER

TOBOGGAN...

T

T-Bar	Mechnical device for tipping two people over in the snow at once.
Tents	Accommodation designed to keep people in a state of back-breaking, frigid intimacy. Gear which looks most romantic viewed through a shop window.
Thaw	Life's like that. Everything melts eventually. Actually you can be thaw in the most amazing places.
Thin	Desperately desired state by slimmers. Desperately undesirable state of the slope.
Toboggan	Expeditious method for descending the slopes *without* expensive ski lessons. Legend has it that the first creature to go tobogganing was a polar bear. When confronted with a snow-covered slope he just sat down on himself and slid.
Tram Lines	Old tracks frozen in the snow. The time when you need a kindly tram conductor.
Traverse	You are moving across the slope with your skis at right angles to the fall line. Skiing is like yachting, nearly always you are moving in a different direction to where you want to go.
Trees	Pretty things which God designed to prevent skiers going too fast in any one direction.
Tuck	That crouched position one gets into when moving at 120 kmh and racing like hell. More sensibly, it is the Mars bar you keep in your parka pocket.

Tuning	Preparing skis by sanding, filing, waxing, rubbing . . . getting the week off, placating your spouse, finding your goggles, getting the parka you lent to your son, putting the rack on the roof, putting in the anti-freeze, borrowing chains, persuading your bank manager . . . tuning can take all summer.
Turkey	An inept skier, invariably yearning for sympathy. He (she) rarely gets it.

U

Underwear	Very fancy indeed. It comes in all colours. It can be electric, it can be thermal, it can be made of new miracle fibres like pyrophobic polypropylene, but somehow the old neck-to-knees that grandfather used to wear are still the best.
Unweighting	The slight upward movement of the body which eases pressure on the skis for the initiation of a turn. The same effect can be achieved by standing up very early during lunch.
Upmanship	Your parka should be slightly frayed around the edges as evidence of long hours of marathon skiing cross-country. It helps too to have faded badges, Grindelwald, Kitzbühle, Aspen, Vale, St Moritz, Naeba and Tyndall Glacier.

TURKEY...

WHITE - OUT...

V

Virgin	Snow that falls pure and untouched over-night. The only thing that does actually.
Visibility	Elusive thing that constantly changes on the mountain from zero to hundreds of kilometres. Often depends on the quality of the juice you have been drinking.

W

Water	Snow that's had a very hard day.
Week-Ends	Times when all the people that you hoped were still in the city are covering the slopes.
Weight Change	Transfer of weight from one ski to another. Or taking your foot off the accelerator at the sight of a police car.
White-Out	Too much whiteness above and below. Alternatively the hideous day one at the beach.
Widow	Either male or female. Inevitably a beautiful understanding creature who doesn't mind a bit when you want to slip away for a week with your mates on a very important errand in the snow.

X

X-Country	Short for cross-country. Actually it never turns out to be short when you are using your own muscle.
X-Ray	Scientific instrument used to discover whether you actually have any bones left.

Y

Yodel	Falsetto cry of extreme elation inevitably perpetrated at 1 am.
Yuppy	One who doesn't wear last year's Porsche or last year's outfit.

Z

Zero	Desirable state of weather. Undesirable state of skier's bank balance.
Ziggy	That lovely man who held your waist so tenderly when you were learning to ski. You never found out his other name.

Zigzagging	A typical downhill skier always zigs before you have a chance to zag.
Zssssss	More delicate than the tone of a Stradivarius violin, the sound to bring tears to your eyes, skis moving sweetly over powder snow.